NUMBERS

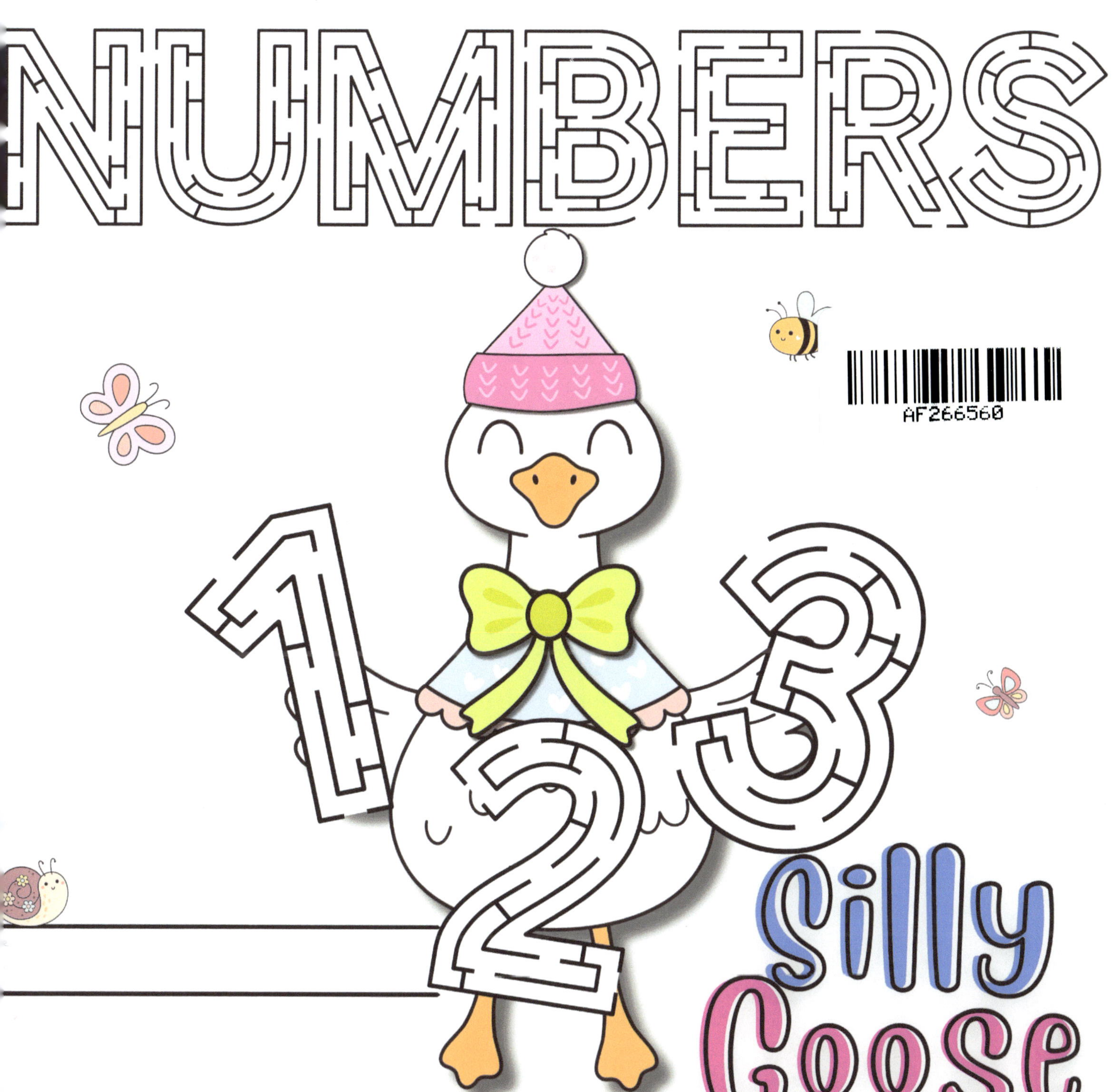

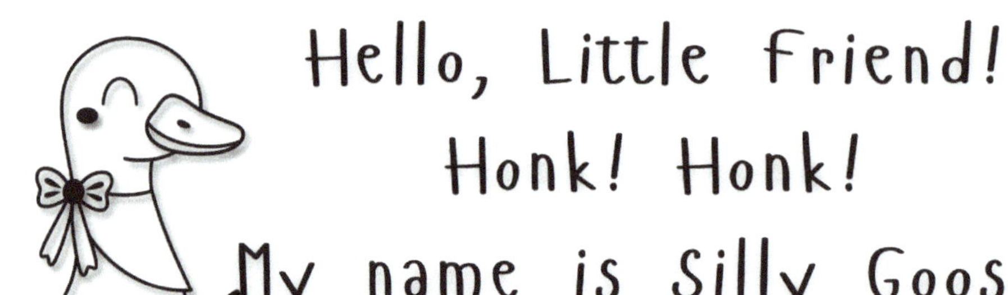

Hello, Little friend!
Honk! Honk!
My name is Silly Goose,
and I love counting!
In this book,
we will learn numbers 1 to 20
together.
You can COUNT the numbers, TRACE
them with your favorite pencil, and
help me
SOLVE FUN MAZES.
Are you ready for a silly counting
adventure?
Let's count, trace, and play!

This book is dedicated to all
Curious Little Learners
who love to count, explore, and
discover new things every day.
And
to the Wonderful Parents and Teachers
who help Children
GROW, LEARN,
and
BELIEVE IN THEMSELVES.
May every Number bring a Smile
and every page sparks
love for learning.

ZAZULEAC WORLD

ISBN: 978-1-957988-10-8

Designed in the U.S.A.

one

two

three

four

Five

six

seven

Amazing
Unique
Loved
Powerful
Valued
Brave
Kind
Happy
eight

nine

ten

twelve

13
thirteen

fourteen

fifteen
15

sixteen
16
MAIL

seventeen

eighteen
18

nineteen

twenty